MW01293761

FOOL PROOF DICTATION

A NO-NONSENSE SYSTEM FOR EFFECTIVE & REWARDING DICTATION

CHRISTOPHER DOWNING

mad devil media

CONTENTS

Foreword   v

PART 1
WHAT TO EXPECT
How This Will Go   3
Tryout #1   6

PART 2
HOW I DICTATE
A Typical Dictation Session   11
Reading Warm-Up   14
Tryout #2   16
Verbalize Session Goals   20
Practical Exercises   22
Tryout #3   24
2 - 5 - 10 - 20 Write Scene   28
Transcribe & Review   33

PART 3
PRACTICAL EXERCISES
Notes About The Exercises   37
Practical Exercise #1: Simple Sentences & Simple Edits   40
Practical Exercise #2: Sentence Variations v.1   44
Practical Exercise #3: Stream of Consciousness   47
Practical Exercise #4: Sentence Variations v.2   50
Practical Exercise #5: Persuasive Letter To A Friend   53
Practical Exercise #6: Sentence Variations v.3   55
Practical Exercise #7: Alternating POVs   57
Practical Exercise #8: 9000 WPH Mayhem   59
Practical Exercise #9: Flash Fiction   62
Practical Exercise #10: Incremental Scenes   64

PART 4
FINAL NOTES

Your Own Consistent Practice   69
250 Prompts!   72
Simple Sentences & Simple Edits   73
Sentence Variations v.1   80
Stream of Consciousness   91
Sentence Variations v.2   93
Persuasive Letter To A Friend   95
Sentence Variations v.3   97
Alternating POVs   99
9000 WPH Mayhem   102
Flash Fiction   104
Incremental Scenes   106

FOREWORD

If there's one thing that's certain about dictation, it's that almost every writer I've ever known who's tried it has given up at some point. They almost always come back, of course, once they realize what an incredible tool dictation can be and they've discovered the reasons for throwing in the towel in the first place.

Sometimes, that was because of accuracy issues (something that I point out in my book, *The Writer's Guide to Training Your Dragon*, is easily fixed). Other times, it was down to their ability to already generate huge word counts through fast typing. A brush with repetitive strain injury (RSI) usually sends the latter running back to Dragon eventually, though.

But the single biggest reason why many writers seem to bail on dictation, despite its incredible benefits, is down to mindset.

I've lost count of the amount of people who have told me they simply can't transition to writing with their mouth instead of their fingers. It's a mental shift, of course, but one that is straightforward enough to overcome. That's where this excellent little book by Christopher Downing comes in.

As writers, we should be used to change. We've gone from quills to pens to typewriters to computers, all against a backdrop of books moving from the printed page to the electronic screen. It's hard to believe that before the iPhone debuted in 2007 and the iPad in 2010, touch was never regarded as a widespread input method. Now, it's ubiquitous and the writing is on the wall. Voice will soon become a normal, everyday input method and it will be *everywhere*. From Alexa in your home to Siri in your car, getting things done with your voice will slowly become the new normal.

For many of us who have been using dictation software for as long as we can remember, this has always been "the next big thing." Once you make the mental leap to use dictation as part of your writing work-flow, it becomes incredibly difficult to switch back to typing alone. And why would you? Dictation is efficient, accurate and can even be good for your health; anything that gets us out of a chair and moving has to be good in itself, right?

The success stories of those who've embraced dictation are wide-spread and inspiring, from people who have overcome crippling RSI or other physical ailments to busy working parents who have managed to write the novel they've always dreamt about in the down-time between the school run or while mowing the lawn. Take a look at the *Dragon Riders* group on Facebook to see hundreds of writers, many bestselling authors, who were once skeptical but now cannot live without the benefits of dictation as part of their writing life.

Bear in mind, you have to commit. This is not something you can dip in and out of – as Christopher outlines in what you are about to read, dictation is something that takes practice before the mental pins click into place. Don't fall into the trap of taking a hybrid approach – put away that keyboard and stop typing. Use dictation whenever and wherever you can, from sending a text to writing an email. These little steps along the way make building up to a novel that much easier.

Embracing dictation isn't a burden or a chore, despite the initial effort to make the transition. As Christopher mentions, his book will give you a one-way ticket "all the way to Awesome Town," but you have to be willing to board the train and, more importantly, go the distance. Once you have, like any life-changing journey, you'll never look back.

Dictation can make you a more efficient writer, of course, but it can also make you a better one. Stop thinking like a typist – you are a storyteller, after all – and you will be already well on your way to dictation Nirvana. *Fool Proof Dictation*, and all the excellent exercises it contains, is certain to get you over the line that little more quickly and painlessly.

Scott Baker
September 2017
www.trainingyourdragon.com

PART 1

WHAT TO EXPECT

HOW THIS WILL GO

This guide will help you develop into a highly productive, dictating writer. You'll learn clear steps, taking yourself toward confident and fluent dictation. You'll track your own progress. And you'll see results immediately.

This book includes the daily method I use while dictating fiction. The equipment. The warm-ups. The timed sessions. And finally, the method for self-evaluation. It's all here. No gimmicks. No fluff. No nonsense.

You're also getting a lot of practical exercises, the backbone of the Fool Proof Dictation system. Like learning any new skill, you'll use these exercises to advance your abilities, training your brain to accept and value its new skill. Much like the writing prompts you might have used in the past, these offer a continual development of your new skill for the rest of your writing career.

How's that sound? Like a lot all at once?

Actually, it's simple. It just took me two years to figure it all out. By now, I can break it down into easy, accessible chunks.

There are a handful of great books on dictation available on Amazon, and if you want to explore all your dictating options, then the reigning guru is Scott Baker, who wrote the foreword, and his *The Writer's Guide to Training Your Dragon*. Any of the available books might serve a purpose for you, and I don't want discredit any of them. But truth is, none helped me create the system I use today, which, more than any other book available, **focuses on the mental process of dictation**. That is, how to get proficient writing with dictation. I don't worry about wrangling my *Dragon*. I don't use an expensive or technically complicated setup. And I sure as heck don't need anyone convincing me that talking is faster than typing. And, well, that takes care of almost all the dictation literature out there.

Enter Fool Proof Dictation.

Here's how this will go. I'll...

1. explain what a typical dictation session looks like,
2. briefly explain the hows & whys of a typical session,
3. lay out all the exercises you'll need to train your brain to begin your own sessions,
4. and finally, supply material to get you honing those skills right away.

You'll complete three "tryouts" early in this book, small glimpses of what you're getting into. I lined them up to provide an optimized, bit-by-bit learning experience of the Fool Proof Dictation system.

This is not, however, a how-to manual for *Dragon* or other dictation services. I use *Dragon's* transcription function exclusively, and that's what I refer to throughout this book. Transcription, as opposed to dictating text directly onto the screen, is a crucial element to what I do and what I'm sharing with you. How to use specific dictation software is something beyond the scope of this book.

As with my other works, I mention books I recommend. I don't know these authors, and I don't make any affiliate cash. I just like them, and I want you to know about them.

Let's get to it. Ready for your first tryout?

TRYOUT #1

HOW FAST IS FAST ENOUGH?

OBJECTIVE

To feel out an appropriate dictation pace.

YOU'LL NEED

- stopwatch (any app will do)

WHAT TO DO

Below is a passage from a fan favorite by Kafka. I want you to time yourself reading it aloud. Take your time. Don't pronounce punctuation. Don't be fancy. Just read. Slowly. You can whisper if you're not alone, but *you must read it aloud*. Your goal is to read it in 2 minutes and 15 seconds. No more. No less. Go.

> One morning, when Gregor Samsa awoke from troubled dreams in his bed, he discovered he'd

transformed into a horrible insect. He lay on his armored back, and if he lifted his head a little he could see his brown belly, slightly domed and divided by arches into stiff sections. The bedding was hardly able to cover it and seemed ready to slide off any moment. His many legs, pitifully thin compared with the size of the rest of him, waved about helplessly as he looked.

"What's happened to me?" he thought.

It wasn't a dream. His room, a proper human room although a little too small, lay peacefully between its four familiar walls. A collection of textile samples lay spread out on the table—Samsa was a traveling salesman—and above it there hung a picture he'd recently cut out of an illustrated magazine and placed in a nice, pretty frame. It showed a lady dressed in a fur hat and fur boa, sitting upright, raising a heavy fur muff that covered the whole of her lower arm aimed at the viewer.

Okay. How'd you do?

If you finished before 2:15, do it again. Slow down. Repeat. Slow down yet again. Do this until you speak slowly enough to finish as close as you can to 2:15.

SELF-EVALUATION

Here's the deal. Reading this passage in 2 minutes and 15 seconds is almost exactly a rate of 5000 words per hour (WPH). For those of you who thought dictation was supposed to feel zippy, this should be a revelation. Because, to most people, 5000 spoken WPH feels, well, painfully slow.

Dictation isn't a race to get words down. By dictating, you're going to reach high word counts. The trick is *quality* words.

Most of this guide focuses on *that*.

So congrats. Now you know what the pace of 5000 WPH sounds like. This will be a huge surprise to most aspiring dictators. This is your target pace. Get comfortable with it. Welcome aboard.

[*Note: I've already wasted too much time reconfiguring sentences to avoid "dictator." At some point, it just needs to be okay with all of us.*]

PART 2

HOW I DICTATE

A TYPICAL DICTATION SESSION

My writing time is limited. I'm a full-time parent to two little kiddos, so when I get scheduled office hours during preschool, I can't waste time. Writer's block isn't an option. I get in, get to work, and get out. How?

By having a productive routine, a consistent dictation session. By sticking to it. By training my brain to know what's coming, so it can go to that creative zone where all the good stuff happens.

Here's a shot of the actual dictation session schedule I've fine-tuned over time. It's tacked on my wall.

```
 9:00  READING WARM-UP
 9:10  VERBALIZE SESSION GOALS
 9:15  PRACTICAL EXERCISES
10:00  2-5-10-20 WRITE SCENE
10:40  TRANSCRIBE & REVIEW
10:50  CLOSE SHOP
```

I'll go over the details of each segment in the coming chapters. However, here are a few points I want to make now.

Notice the session schedule includes a lot of not-writing. Surprise. I've experimented with variations of my schedule, and I learned that revving up my brain *before* I dictate scenes is invaluable, like playing scales and etudes on the piano before a recital. Every time I think, "Hey, I got this," and skip warm ups, I'm disappointed with my progress. I've learned my lesson. Warming up the dictation part of my noggin is time well spent.

I customized this session schedule for a two-hour window. It allows me to add ~1800 reliable words to a 1st Draft, each session, every day. Needs and opportunities sometimes vary, however. On rare days when my office time gains an hour, I slide in two extra "Write Scene" segments, with breaks in between, allowing for nearly ~5000 words in three hours. That's livable.

During weeks when I'm focused on outlining or editing instead of scene writing, I still do practical exercises for thirty minutes daily. I wouldn't skip them. All sorts of creative ideas come from them, like doodling, and my dictation proficiency continues increasing.

When you plan your own dictation session schedules, rest assured you don't need a lot of time to become a productive writer. Two hours a day, five days a week, will allow you, with a good outline, to knock out the 1st Draft of a novel in less than 25 days. Or three hours a day, two days a week, will get you pretty darn close.

Why not four hour sessions, then? Well, there's this thing called The Law of Diminishing Returns. It says, and I'll paraphrase here, 5000 words a day is great, so you should just go play outside before the quality of your output goes to crap. Therefore, I don't do more than three hours even if I can. I respect The Law. But you do what you want.

Here are the tools I use during a typical session in my office:

- Nuance's *Dragon* software, exclusively its transcription function
- a $16 Logitech headset w/ noise cancelation and a 6' cord
- a higher quality Mp3/voice recorder app ($5) on either my phone or my laptop
- a timer app
- a tracking spreadsheet
- the book I'm currently reading in my genre
- a puzzle, a coloring book, a flipping coin, or a clear path to pace

I also need privacy. The fear of someone eavesdropping while I dictate is a total deal killer. Not an uncommon plight, I suspect. When my home office isn't working for me, I park my car around the corner from the coffee shop and dictate in my front seat if it's not too hot. While I do appreciate my precious writing space when I get it, it's good to be flexible, to have a backup space already planned out.

Another very important point: I take little 3-5 minute breaks between segments within my sessions. However! I don't open any other apps. I don't check email. I don't check my sales report page. I don't get anywhere near the internet. **A dictation session is about immersive creativity, and I don't want anything bringing me out of that state.** Breaks include walking around my office, improvising on my violin, staring out the window, staring at the ceiling, using the bathroom, refilling my coffee, stretching. I could spend an entire chapter stressing this, but I won't, so just heed my point. Take breaks, and be deliberate about what they should and shouldn't be.

Now, let's deconstruct what goes into each segment of a session, each line in my session schedule, so you can begin formulating your own.

READING WARM-UP

- I spend ten minutes reading aloud from a book in my genre, punctuation and all, usually on my feet, pacing slowly, heel-toe, heel-toe.

At this point in my practice, I can sense a 5000 WPH pace, and I make sure I'm reading slowly and thoughtfully. For a time, I recorded, transcribed, and logged my reading times, pursuing 5000 WPH until I internalized the timing. Again this is *my* optimum pace, and you may find that your own is different. But 5000 WPH is a great target for beginners.

Reading aloud is one of the easiest things you can do to become a better dictator. The effort/reward ratio is way up there.

When I was first learning to dictate, I stayed away from reading aloud as a practical exercise. I figured I was supposed to be training the *composition* part of my brain, not the reading part. Turns out, I didn't know what I was talking about. Because truth is, the brain is a complicated beast, and everything is interconnected. It listens to the audible voice. It makes adjustments. It notes patterns. It learns from an unfathomable amount of input. It is pretty cool.

Reading aloud at the beginning of a session prepares me for dictation. Here's how.

1. Reading aloud sets the pace. I shoot for 5000 WPH because it's my optimum productivity pace. As I read aloud, I remind myself to go slow, to drop in little pauses before and after punctuation, to notice rhythms and variations of sentences, to breathe. (No coincidence, I'm a follower of Chris Fox. I listened to his 5000 *Words Per Hour* the same year I started figuring all this out. The title of his book is also no coincidence.)
2. Reading aloud rouses the language centers of the brain. There's some Pavlovian science happening too, signaling my head that it's show time.
3. Reading aloud develops verbal agility, especially with genre lingo and descriptors I don't use in daily conversation. It also keeps me comfortable with dictating simple punctuation.
4. Reading aloud gets me cozy with my headset. It doesn't always feel natural.

Frankly, it's just a great way to start. I like the no-pressure feel. It's part of the job, but it doesn't feel like work.

Let's get you set up, so you can begin tracking yourself and developing the comfort of speaking at your own optimal pace. Will it be 5000 WPH? You won't know until you log some legitimate hours dictating. But it's a great pace to aim for.

Onward to another tryout!

TRYOUT #2

READING WARM-UP

OBJECTIVE

To ease into dictation with a calm, effective warm-up, speaking slowly and clearly, gaining comfort with punctuation.

YOU'LL NEED

- *Dragon* for Mac or PC
- noise cancelation headset microphone, non-bluetooth
- high bit-rate Mp3 voice recorder app
- word processor with a word count feature
- stopwatch
- tracking spreadsheet from
  foolproofdictation.wordpress.com
- current bestseller from your genre

Now's the time to get Nuance's *Dragon* if you haven't yet, available for both PC and Mac. It's pricey. It's an investment you need to be serious about. There is, however, a 30-day guarantee, so there's no risk having it long enough to get you through this book. Yes, there's a way to finagle Google's Voice Typing to transcribe audio files, and I've done it, but *Dragon*, even with its imperfections, gets the job done best. I haven't even upgraded to v.6 for Mac.

Please note that not all versions of *Dragon* offer a transcribing feature, so explore until you find one that does. Transcription, the process of converting audio recordings into text, is the only method I use for dictation. Dictating text directly onto the screen tends to create more errors, and more importantly, worrying about *Dragon's* accuracy while composing fiction is detrimental to the creative process.

Also, there's some great, cheap, noise cancelling microphones out there. No need to break the bank. You should get a headset with a boom mic and a long cord, so you can move about worry-free. Bluetooths are a no-go. I've used my $16 Logitech headset (AMZN ID: B003H4QPJQ) for more than a year without replacement, *and* I see the price has come down even more, so hurray for you.

As for the voice recorder app, explore your options. Your phone probably came with a voice recorder, but drop $5 on a better app with good reviews, both for your phone and your computer. I've never had an issue with a mono Mp3 format at 224Kbps, but I've observed *Dragon* fuddle up M4As. I record directly to my laptop almost exclusively.

The tracking spreadsheet, found at foolproofdictation.wordpress.com, is an *Excel* file, but it's basic enough to open in *Numbers* (for Mac) without trouble.

WHAT TO DO

Record yourself reading aloud from a current bestseller in your genre for 10 minutes.

Include all punctuation *except quotation marks.* Say "new line" at the beginning of every paragraph. Skip emphasis fonts, such as italics, underlines, and caps.

If you make a mistake, then pause, say "whoops," pause again, and start the sentence over. If the mistake was especially dreadful, start the whole paragraph over.

If you need to, stop talking and let the recorder keep going. Sip a beverage. Catch your breath. Roll your neck around. A 15 second blank space in your recording won't harm the transcription process.

Then via *Dragon,* transcribe your audio to your word processor. Don't stress over accuracy yet, but take a peek where *Dragon* got it right and where it didn't. You might even listen along once you see the transcription, noting where you could have articulated better. But don't fret. Yet.

Log your time and your word count on the spreadsheet.

SELF-EVALUATION

Measure and track yourself reading aloud for a month. A few times per day if you can. For now, strive for that slow, lulling 5000 WPH. You don't get extra points for higher word counts. On the contrary, you win the game by speaking clearly, slowly, and consistently.

Check in with yourself. Your breathing. Your anxiety. The confidence in your voice. The *lack* of confidence in your voice.

You'll probably need some practice. That's okay. I needed lots.

This exercise alone will resolve most accuracy issues. Enjoy it.

[Note: *If you're wondering why I only use transcription and never, never, never live-dictate directly onto the screen, then here's your chance to find out. Read the same passage aloud in dictation mode. See for yourself how much fun it is. Enough said.*]

VERBALIZE SESSION GOALS

- I spend 5 minutes dictating what I want to achieve this session.

No big secrets here.

This does two things. It connects the language composition part of my brain to my mouth, and it clarifies and solidifies my intentions for roughly the next two hours.

I like to set aside all the chatter in my head that prevents me from focusing on the task at hand. If my priority for a dictation session is getting out a particular scene, then I state that. I also usually reaffirm my desire to improve both my writing and dictation skills. And I verbalize all the whys. Specific goal-setting pushes all the other worries, like the rest of the novel, far into the periphery.

This may seem silly to some. Works great for me.

I'd do this longhand even if I wasn't dictating. It's a great productivity enhancer for any endeavor. Like reviewing the agenda at the beginning of a meeting, it keeps all the scatter-brained employees from getting off topic.

I rarely transcribe this, but I often record it. Makes it feel super-duper official.

PRACTICAL EXERCISES

- I spend 40 minutes practicing different techniques and variations of dictation, sometimes relevant to my work in progress (WIP), sometimes not.
- While I dictate, I distract myself by coloring, fiddling with a hand-held puzzle, pacing the room, or flipping a coin.
- Between types of exercises, I take a 5-minute break.

Over the past two years, I've compiled a list of practical exercises that helped me develop my dictation skills. There's only 10 of them, but the results are infinitely variable. I've done thousands of exercises by now, and I've never felt they were repetitive.

Two exercises are my favorites because I get the most out of them. But to enforce variety, I've plugged my list of exercises into a random decision maker app. It decides which two forms of mental calisthenics I do each day. I like that randomness and surprise. I think it's good for me, being a big control freak. Then again, sometimes I simply know what I need for the day. And I do it. Because I'm the boss.

Types of practical exercises include:

- repeating and developing the same scene with incrementally longer dictations
- dictating varieties of sentence construction
- paddling down streams of consciousness
- describing a setting via alternating POV characters
- dictating as quickly as I can
- composing flash fiction

I'll complete this list and go over each thoroughly in later chapters. But you get the idea.

Some exercises are harder than others. One can be fun. Then the next day, the same one is hellish. More often than not, my own headspace is what's different. So I use these practical exercises not only to get better at dictating but also to get my head on straight. They prepare me for the real writing ahead. Days when exercises seem difficult remind me just how important warm-up is. **Writing scenes with the wrong mindset is torture. Practical exercises help fix that**.

If I only have thirty minutes to dictate on a given day, I commit ten of them toward proper warm-up, including at least a brief attempt at one of the practical exercises.

Ready to start getting serious? Your next tryout is one of my favorite exercises.

TRYOUT #3

INCREMENTAL SCENES

OBJECTIVE

To experience the best exercise for creating dictation proficiency.

YOU'LL NEED

- your dictation setup: *Dragon*, mic, voice recorder, word processor
- stopwatch
- tracking spreadsheet

WHAT TO DO

Dictate a scene using a simple outline, expanding its details and length in incremental rounds. The first round is 2 minutes. The second is 3 minutes. And the third is 5 minutes.

This is one of the ten practical exercises I use to gain proficiency at dictation. It's my favorite. I believe it's the best at organizing all the components, all the brain parts, into a larger cohesive machine. You're going to jump right in and try it out early because it'll give you an abbreviated sense of what you can do.

Below is a scene outline, bare-bones and full of opportunity for your own imagination. It's not meant to help you win any awards, so embrace its simplicity. Imagine it as a single, very short scene within the context of a larger story. You'll barely get a few hundred words.

Prompt

- **Scene Summary:** Little Red Riding Hood is trying to get to grandma's house, but she's convinced by the sly wolf to go into the woods and pick more flowers.
- **Where:** Dark, misty forest
- **Opening:** LRRH rushed down the path, worrying about grandma.
- **Peak Emotional Moment:** LRRH went against her better judgement and did what the wolf said, wasting time picking flowers for grandma.
- **Ending:** LRRH rushed down the path again, the creatures of the forest chastising her for all the right reasons.

Step 1. Imagine the scene chronologically in your head. Close your eyes and visualize the entire short scene, beginning to end, *through the eyes of the POV character*, generating the scene's details as you go. Do this two times.

[*Visualizing the scene "through the eyes of the POV character" will be new to most. It works wonders.*]

Step 2. Start the recorder. Set the timer for 2 minutes. Dictate the scene using the basic outline as best as you can, filling in setting details, character details, and other actions as you go. Stay calm. Speak slowly. But cut yourself off when the timer buzzes, finished or not. This will get a little messy. Don't transcribe anything yet. Instead, take a minute to wiggle your limbs.

[*As with the previous tryout, include all punctuation except quotation marks. Say "new line" at the beginning of every paragraph. Skip emphasis fonts, such as italics, underlines, and caps. If you make a mistake, then pause, say "whoops," pause again, and start the sentence over. Removing mistakes later while editing at the keyboard, those marked in your text by that "whoops," is a simple task.*]

Step 3. This time, set the timer for 3 minutes. Dictate the scene again. Use those details from step two that you remember, that stood out. Now you have more time to squeeze in a proper ending, more valuable details, more actions that speak to the characters' motivations. Try your best to speak at that slow 5000 WPH pace. At the buzzer, stop and shake it off. Still no transcribing.

Step 4. Set the timer for 5 minutes. Dictate the scene again. But this time, try to have fun. Breathe. Enlarge one scene beat. Shrink another. Feel it out. Use details you remember from the other two steps. Don't worry if you can't recall them all. That's one of the reasons you're recording. Create more details and more actions to fill in the time. Don't go past the buzzer.

Step 5. Transcribe all three attempts. Log word counts. Don't worry if the transcriptions aren't perfect. No need to edit them. This isn't about achieving accuracy. It's about organizing your thoughts. It's about composing verbally. Besides, this is just a tryout.

SELF-EVALUATION

Well, if these were your first attempts at dictating scenes, your results were probably rough at best. Just typing the instructions gave me nervous flashbacks to my first tries at this exercise, which were laughable. By the end of the second or third time, however, I knew in my gut I was onto something.

Did it feel like fun for you? I hope so.

Did having a basic outline help, giving you a place to start, a milestone in the middle, and an ending to aim for?

Did you get tongue-tied? Did you draw blanks? Did you completely fail to wrap up the scene even at 5 minutes? It'd be amazing if you answered no to all three of these questions at this point.

You should now have a sense that **gradually increasing the time you dictate, thus gradually increasing your own expectations, also improves your mental grip on the scene**, more than if you started at 5 minutes.

Once you've taken a break, try it again while doodling simple shapes on a sheet of paper. If you're opposed to doodling, find something to do with your hands or feet. The point is to distract yourself *just enough* to interfere with your inner critic. Eventually, you'll pick your own method, but I swear this technique works like a charm. One of my favorites is dictating on my feet while repeatedly flipping and catching a coin. Another is coloring my daughter's *Trolls* coloring book. Another is pacing slowly, consciously lining up my feet as I go.

Ultimately, when you begin writing real scenes in your novels, you'll be dictating nearly 20-minute sessions, potentially 1500-word scenes. Building scenes incrementally, using an outline, is what Fool Proof Dictation is all about.

In the next chapter, I'll show you how I expand on this practical exercise and use it to write *for reals*.

2 - 5 - 10 - 20 WRITE SCENE

- I generate the 1st Draft of a scene from my WIP, first visualizing it several times, then dictating the scene incrementally.

This is where I work on my novel. This is where all the payoff comes from the earlier warm-up and practice.

It's go time.

For roughly 40 minutes, I dictate a single scene using a method very similar to Tryout #3. Using my outline, I first visualize the scene multiple times as if I'm in the head of the POV character. Then, I begin dictating the scene, expanding it in incrementally larger rounds of time. Those rounds are 2, 5, 10, and 20 minutes. And I use some method of distraction the whole time.

I first started dictating scenes this way after reading Rachel Aaron's ***2k to 10k: Writing Faster, Writing Better, and Writing More of What You Love***. Although she wasn't writing about dictation, she convinced me to compose a brief summary of a scene before writing it all the way through. This step alone helped me write more efficiently at the keyboard by leaps and bounds.

When I began dictating instead of typing, I still did this summarization—only verbally. Then, I increased the length of the summary, adding more details. Then, I increased it again. And again. Next thing I knew, I wasn't summarizing the scene. I was dictating the whole thing—almost with ease. And, presto, that's how Fool Proof Dictation was born.

Even now, the first 2-minute round is barely more than that 250-word summary of my scene. To begin with, I use a scene synopsis notecard with its significant elements, identical to the scene outline from Tryout #3.

Then, each progressive round incorporates more and more details, most of which have already been hashed out in a more detailed outline during my prewriting phase.

After I've finished the long 20-minute round, I transcribe all four rounds. Then, I quickly compile them into a single, full-length 1st Draft of the scene. Usually takes me 5 minutes of cut and pasting with some minor touch ups. Two years ago, this step took 30 minutes, but it shrunk with practice.

The punctuation instructions from Tryouts #2 and #3 are those I use for myself. I don't dictate quotation marks during dialogue, just the commas. While I don't even notice "period" and "comma," the words "open quote/close quote" fumble my flow, and dialogue, if it's going to be good, is where I need my creative flow to be uninterrupted. I add quotation marks during my second or third editing pass.

As I instructed you to do earlier, if I make a mistake, I say "whoops," which marks the mistake and can be easily searched for later, and I start the sentence over. "Whoops" is a silly word I use for a reason. It keeps mistakes from feeling too heavy.

Here's an important point. If, for example, I don't like something in my 5-minute round, I merely leave it out or replace it when I dictate my 10-minute round. In other words, I don't dictate my 5-minute round twice because I didn't like it. I mentally note what to change. Then, I change it as I move on, **keeping the creative momentum moving forward**.

After all, this is just the 1st Draft of the scene. It's not supposed to be perfect. It is, however, supposed to be moving in the right direction. So I keep moving. With time and practice, I've learned to trust my imagination, my outline, and my forthcoming editing enough to keep riding the wave of creativity in the moment.

In addition to the scene synopsis notecard I use for the first round of my scene, the same one featured in Tryout #3, I also outline each scene in further detail during prewriting. My detailed outline includes all the crucial character and setting notes I need, laid out chronologically. As my rounds of dictation increase for each scene, much of what I'm adding is already on hand in the outline right in front of me, thanks to prewriting, providing a list of milestones to keep my scene on track.

Dictating an entire scene with no plan? That's a disaster waiting to happen. Dictating a scene from my detailed outline? It feels a lot like merely connecting the dots. Hell, anyone can do that. Even me.

For your own practice, you'll need to find a novel and scene outlining system that works for you. Experiment with outlines of varying detail. It should contain enough information about your scene that you can expand your own scenes in incremental rounds. **Don't count on improvising details while dictating**. Sometimes it works. Most of the time it doesn't, and it bogs down your dictation session, and in the long run, you'll grow frustrated. Again, don't dictate a scene, incrementally or not, without some sort of outline.

This may be bad news for writers who prefer not to outline and plan ahead.

I always start with at least the synopsis notecard, listed immediately below, which is the bare minimum and perhaps all you may need. Further below, you'll see the questionnaire I use to build my own detailed outlines at the scene level. The book **Fool Proof Outline** offers in-depth commentary and instructions for my outlining system, but it's not necessary for everybody. It's just what works for me.

SYNOPSIS NOTECARD

- Scene Summary (*incl. POV character's goal*):
- Where:
- Opening:
- Peak Emotional Moment:
- Ending:

SCENE BASICS

- Who was the POV character?
- What was POV doing at the beginning?
- What did POV need?
- List the other characters in the scene, along with their wants during the scene?
- Who or what obstructed POV's need?
- List the times this happens:
- What was the moment & emotion of peak intensity?
- What concerns were raised by the end?
- What was POV doing at the end, showing that concern?

SETTING

- Brainstorm vivid details that show time, place, weather, & culture *from POV's perspective*:

- List at least a few moments when POV physically interacted with the environment:
- What setting details mirrored the tension and/or theme?
- What objects revealed details about plot & character?
- List a few mundane details that engaged POV's senses, creating a sense of realism:

CHARACTERS & PLOT

- How did POV *actively* move the plot forward?
- List specific visceral/somatic responses to emotions or actions, *especially* for the moment of peak intensity:
- How did POV's character flaw show up?
- How was POV forced to reevaluate or change?

DRAMATIC TENSION

- How did danger or demise loom (*physical, psychological, or professional*)?
- Brainstorm at least two unexpected ways to show tension in the scene:

EXTRA STUFF

- What opening hook lured POV (*and reader*) deeper into the scene?
- What was the prompt to the next scene?
- What fascinating idea, fact, or event was teased to come later, even subtly?
- What specific actions furthered subplots, w/o being mere exposition or an info-dump?
- What was the unexplained, unexpected event, action, or item that will surprise the reader?
- How was the theme challenged or championed?

TRANSCRIBE & REVIEW

- I transcribe any remaining recordings.
- I log all my times, word counts, and types of dictation/exercise.
- I make notes—mental or written—about what worked this session, what didn't, and what tweaks I might make next time.

Watching my word counts gradually increase along with the quality of my work, that combo is hard to beat. Measurable progress. Hard-earned gains.

Logging my long-term trends also gives me hope during what I call J-curve weeks, temporary slumps I rise out of better than before. When my WPH, scene quality, or even morale dips, then I set aside my WIP, focus on practical exercises for a week, and end up a better dictator/writer than I was before the slump. Because I'm human, slumps cause me to lose focus on the long-term improvements. If not for the spreadsheet, I'd just mope, drink too much coffee, and get snappy with my kids. True story.

To this day, I log most of my exercises. Definitely my scene work. I don't have a contract, a manager, an agent, or a supervising editor looming over me. So this is simply me being honest with myself. I know I can get lazy or moody. I need some accountability. The spreadsheet helps.

I've added and subtracted columns from the sheet over the last two years. The one whose web address is listed in Tryout #2 is the version I always return to. It's simple. It measures things I want to improve. It gets the job done.

PART 3

PRACTICAL
EXERCISES

NOTES ABOUT THE EXERCISES

Coming up, I'll lay out all the practical exercises that will take even the most hesitant, fumbling dictator all the way to Awesome Town. One way ticket. You just need to get on the train.

Learning to dictate your novel involves more than learning how to dictate scenes. In fact, most people who try dictation usually give up in frustration because they focus on their WIP. The Fool Proof Dictation system splits your dictation sessions, half on your WIP, half developing the capacity to dictate comfortably and effectively. In my experience, you need both halves in order to succeed long-term as a dictator.

Said differently, these practical exercises serve your WIP as much as they serve you.

The next 10 chapters lay out the exercises. After each exercise is explained, there's a single prompt for you to try out. Then, in the back of this book, you'll find a hefty amount of supplemental prompts to keep you going for months.

When you're beginning your own dictation practice, download a random decision maker app, plug in the names of the exercises, and let the universe decide which 2 you'll do each dictation session. Random selection keeps you from staying in your comfort zone. Like me, you'll never regret having to do those exercises you don't favor. **You, your WIP, and your readers will benefit from them all.**

During your future dictation sessions, you'll do as many prompts as time allows, usually only 2 or 3 per exercise.

You're going to focus a lot on sentences. In dictation, there's no better tool than the sentence, and you must know, without a doubt, how to use this tool. You must be in control of sentences. You must know their various structures, their potential, their pitfalls. More than anything you dictate, you must use them well. A remarkable little ebook by Charles Euchner, *Sentences and Paragraphs*, says:

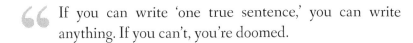 If you can write 'one true sentence,' you can write anything. If you can't, you're doomed.

You won't need to nerd-out like I do on the subject, but you need to understand things like independent clauses, modifiers, and adverbial phrases.

In the long-run, your dictation practice will thrive if you chow down on some technical knowledge of sentence construction. At some point, maybe not right now, grab a book on the subject. I highly recommend the second half of Barbara Baig's, *Spellbinding Sentences*. After that, work through chapters 5-7 from Brooks Landon's *Building Great Sentences*.

The following exercises build upon each other, both linearly and circularly. That way, once you've developed some momentum with some regular sessions, they'll all work together for you no matter what order you complete them.

Some prompts are intentionally goofy. They're there to keep you from getting weighed down by your own expectations. They're there to remind you that practical exercises aren't for the public. They're there to jolt you out of your own headspace, which sometimes gets too cluttered to dictate well. A nonsense scene about a talking rabbit and a traveling vacuum salesman is just the thing. Trust me. So embrace the goofy ones when they show up, okay? Even Hemingway had a sense of humor.

In the end, any conventional writing prompt will get you dictating. Books of writing prompts are everywhere. Half of them are actually good. Use them. The exercises and prompts included in the Fool Proof Dictation system, however, will expedite your development, touching on specific avenues of dictation fluency. They work.

Finally, the goal of these next chapters isn't mastering any one exercise or any one style of prompt or any one scene. The goal is dictating well. Be okay with the struggle and the imperfect results of the exercises. You'll be moving in the right direction.

Let's take a look now.

PRACTICAL EXERCISE #1: SIMPLE SENTENCES & SIMPLE EDITS

OBJECTIVE

To develop trust in your editing. To free yourself from any hindering expectations of fancy-schmancy dictation.

YOU'LL NEED

- your dictation setup: *Dragon*, mic, voice recorder, word processor

WHAT TO DO

Using the words in the prompt, improvise 10-15 *narrative* sentences within your genre, sentences that use only a subject and a verb phrase. No conjunctions. No commas.

The verb phrase may, however, contain a preposition and/or a direct object.

Examples of simple sentences:

1. The agent was nervous.
2. The agent hid his face.
3. The agent used a newspaper.
4. The newspaper was wet and soggy.
5. The agent moved across the street.
6. The agent looked over his shoulder.
7. The rain was too loud.
8. His heart began to race.
9. There was nowhere to hide.
10. Water sloshed up his pants.
11. The water was dirty.
12. The sidewalk stretched along the building.
13. The agent hated being exposed.

Each sentence is its own idea. Modifiers, such as adjectives, get their own sentence, as in the case of the wet, soggy newspaper.

Dictating effective simple sentences will make you a better dictator because there's no pressure to be clever. **Your ideas are less likely to get muddled on their way out from the creative centers of your brain**. It's actually easier to drift into a creative flow state dictating simple sentences once you get the hang of it. You're just getting ideas out, hopefully in some narrative order.

The most important part of this practical exercise, however, is what you do with those simple sentences, the editing. You need to trust that you'll be able to edit those simple sentences into more appealing sentences, or at least a workable 1st Draft.

Two examples of editing:

 The agent hid his face behind a wet, soggy newspaper.

Nervous, he moved across the street, looking over his shoulder, knowing he shouldn't. The rain was loud. His heart began racing, for there was nowhere to hide. Dirty water sloshed up his pants as he peered down the sidewalk, which stretched along the building. He hated being so exposed.

...or...

 The agent was nervous enough to try hiding behind the newspaper, too wet and soggy to do much good. Instead, she moved across the street, dirty rainwater sloshing up her stockings. She looked over her shoulder, knowing there was nowhere to hide. Despite the loud rain, she could hear her heart racing in her ears. She dreaded the sidewalk stretching along the building. She hated being this exposed.

Dictate simple sentences. Trust that you'll edit them well later. This is a liberating process.

You could write the 1st Draft of an entire scene this way. In fact, it's not the worst way to do it, especially if you're having a rough dictation day. Edit it later. Clean it up and add style tomorrow. It's a legitimate technique to keep up momentum.

Try the prompt below. Roll the words around in your imagination for a moment. Then, dictate a narrative paragraph made up of 10-15 simple sentences. There's no timer. There's no race. Work within your genre. It's okay if your narrative becomes a tad nonsensical.

Then, transcribe and edit them into two versions (as above) with your keyboard. That's where the quality comes from.

You can, in the future, time yourself and log word counts.

Here you go.

PROMPT

- impoverished musician
- jewelry box
- torn carpet
- love note
- lighter

[You get bonus points for thinking beyond the obvious in these kinds of prompts. A love letter and a lighter? What's predictable? Sheesh. Avoid that.]

PRACTICAL EXERCISE #2:
SENTENCE VARIATIONS V.1

OBJECTIVE

To develop a controlled rhythm of dictation, using both simple and compound sentences.

YOU'LL NEED

- your dictation setup: *Dragon*, mic, voice recorder, word processor

WHAT TO DO

In a *descriptive* paragraph, dictate four simple sentences, followed by a longer compound sentence. Or reversing the order, start with the compound sentence, followed by four short simple ones.

Compound sentences are two independent clauses, each with their own subject and verb phrase, often separated by a comma and a conjunction.

Here are two examples of the result:

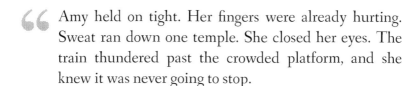 Amy held on tight. Her fingers were already hurting. Sweat ran down one temple. She closed her eyes. The train thundered past the crowded platform, and she knew it was never going to stop.

...or alternately...

Goldilocks bolted upright in the bed, but her eyes refused to open. The floorboards squeaked. She felt frozen. She wasn't alone. She smelled bear.

Beginning with shorter, simple sentences can serve as a brainstorm, a build-up of ideas and observations. The longer compound sentence is the strong finale. (S-S-S-L)

Alternately, beginning with the longer sentence makes a strong stance. The following shorter sentences, then, are a barrage of supporting facts. (L-S-S-S)

You may do this already as a writer. Good. Converting this same skill to dictation will come *slightly* easier.

Just so you know, we're not trying to cover all constructions of compound sentences. Nor will we, in later exercises, cover all constructions of more complicated sentences. This isn't a grammar tutorial. We're simply discussing a few easy examples, following the purpose of our objective stated above. (By the way, that was L-L-S-L.)

Prompts for this practical exercise will be pictures. Describing a static image is surprisingly difficult. Instead, quickly conjure a little narrative behind the image. Describe what you're seeing in the moment of that narrative. That's how we writers think, anyway.

Begin incorporating this controlled, alternating rhythm of sentences during your future dictations and exercises. **You'll not only dictate with greater style, but you'll maintain greater control of your creative thoughts as you dictate.**

Transcribe your paragraphs after you've completed several for the image. Give them a quick keyboard edit for clarity. Little edits, as in the previous exercise, will give you clues to improve by.

You can, in the future, time yourself and log word counts.

Start here.

PROMPT

PRACTICAL EXERCISE #3: STREAM OF CONSCIOUSNESS

OBJECTIVE

To increase your comfort during dictation by removing all expectations of composition other than complete sentences.

YOU'LL NEED

- your dictation setup: *Dragon*, mic, voice recorder, word processor
- stopwatch
- tracking spreadsheet
- your distraction of choice (coin, doodling paper, Rubik's cube, etc.)

WHAT TO DO

Dictate a 10-minute stream of consciousness, beginning with the subject of the prompt. Say whatever you want. Go where your brain wants you to go. Get off topic. Stay on topic. Doesn't matter.

Promise yourself no one will ever read this stuff.

The only requirement is that you don't stop dictating. If you draw a blank, describe the room around you or how you feel. Anything. There's no need for paragraphs breaks, either. Just use "period" and "comma."

If you've never completed streams of consciousness, you'll find they're more difficult than they sound. But they get easier and more fluid, even dream-like, over time.

If your stream of consciousness comes out too organized, then you're probably restricting yourself too much. Control freaks like me have trouble with this. Maybe you'll need practice letting go too. That's okay. It's good for us.

If you're currently working on a novel, consider doing some of these within the head of your characters, using his/her voice the whole time. Who knows what surprises await?

Remember to speak slowly and clearly, even if you get on a roll. Hover around your optimized dictation pace, of which you should have a inkling by now.

Start your recorder.

Start the 10-minute timer.

Grab your distraction.

And above all, relax. See where your mind goes.

PROMPT

- Why is a particular book or movie one of your favorites?

PRACTICAL EXERCISE #4: SENTENCE VARIATIONS V.2

OBJECTIVE

To develop further agility with sentence rhythms and variations, this time adding modifying phrases.

YOU'LL NEED

- your dictation setup: *Dragon*, mic, voice recorder, word processor

WHAT TO DO

In a *narrative* paragraph, dictate the events surrounding the situational prompt, using four short simple sentences and one expanded sentence, specifically one with dependent modifiers. It doesn't matter what order they go in, as long as you're deliberate.

In case you need brushing up, here are few examples of...

...simple sentences:

- The driver lumbered away from the truck.
- Her house felt alive.
- My dog won't forgive me.

...and expanded sentences:

- The driver lumbered away from the truck, old, broken, and, like the truck, without a future.
- Her house felt alive, bustling with three daughters and all their friends.
- Wide-eyed and drooling, my dog won't forgive me, the greedy hoarder of pizza.

Simply put, the sentences of the second set contain additional descriptive phrases, separated by commas, that cannot stand on their own because they don't contain both a noun and verb, or either.

Don't get hung up on the grammar. That's not the point. This is dictation practice, not a grammar quiz. Merely expand the idea of a simple sentence with descriptions set apart by commas. Easy. **This structure creates a rhythm that your dictating brain can latch onto, and the alternating sentence length creates a rhythm your readers will latch onto too.** Everybody wins.

Try out this prompt.

In a single paragraph, what events, big or small, surrounded this situation?

PROMPT

- Selena was nervous about her upcoming speech. John didn't want her to go through with it.

PRACTICAL EXERCISE #5:
PERSUASIVE LETTER TO A FRIEND

OBJECTIVE

To dictate passionately while maintaining the same slow, articulate pace.

YOU'LL NEED

- your dictation setup: *Dragon*, mic, voice recorder, word processor
- stopwatch
- your distraction of choice

WHAT TO DO

Dictate a *persuasive* letter to a fictitious friend for 10 minutes.

To keep this from becoming a stream of consciousness rant, state your stance near the beginning of the letter. Then, follow with separate paragraphs to make your case, point by point.

This is a *Persuasive Letter To A Friend* because you don't want to fret over formalized sentences and fancy words. Also, because if I titled this practical exercise *5 Paragraph Essay*, no one would do it. Not even me.

To make this even more worry-free, the prompts will be bogus, probably nothing you'd ever argue over. Pretend your fictitious friend has made the prompted statement. Then, dictate a letter either agreeing or disagreeing with him. Fake as much passion as you can. Fake your facts. Fake your credentials.

Use the usual punctuation guidelines while dictating. Keep an eye on the timer. Near the 9-minute mark, begin wrapping it up. Don't forget your greeting and closing!

Transcribe and log your words counts.

Now, get revved up. Because your opinion matters!

PROMPT

At last evening's dinner, your friend made the following statement. It's kept you up all night. Do you agree or disagree?

- Weekends are for wimps!

PRACTICAL EXERCISE #6:
SENTENCE VARIATIONS V.3

OBJECTIVE

To maintain control while dictating longer sentences.

YOU'LL NEED

- your dictation setup: *Dragon*, mic, voice recorder, word processor
- a single 6-sided die (or a dice rolling app)

WHAT TO DO

Roll the die. The resulting number, 1-6, is the amount of sentences you'll use for your paragraph.

Compose a *narrative* paragraph in 1st person, relating how you (yes, you specifically) complete the task determined by the prompt.

The length of your paragraph is up to you, but you'll need to use enough words to tell your narrative. A lower number of sentences, such as 1 or 2, forces you to compose cumulative sentences logically stacked with free modifiers, appositives, and independent clauses. A higher number of sentences, on the other hand, allows for variety, and you can decide how to order the differing lengths. Both outcomes are opportunities to dally in rhythm and emphasis.

To compensate for these variables, which can, I'll admit, twist up a beginner's noodle, the subject of your paragraphs will be simple daily activities.

Give each prompt several tries, varying the pattern of sentences you use. Feel which work best, which create build up, and which offer resolution. Ultimately, feel which work best to convey your narrative. Try rolling the die a few times for each prompt.

The more you do this, the easier it'll get. **And you'll squirm less with sentence construction where it affects you most, in the middle of composing an actual scene of your novel.**

Transcribe your paragraphs.

Then, edit them on the keyboard, tweaking the sentences, if you can, into a more meaningful narrative, noting how and where your dictation could have been better.

Also, try to emphasize mundane details that reveal something about you, that add personal meaning.

PROMPT

How do you...

...tidy up the living room?

PRACTICAL EXERCISE #7:
ALTERNATING POVS

OBJECTIVE

To develop POV awareness while dictating.

YOU'LL NEED

- your dictation setup: *Dragon*, mic, voice recorder, word processor
- stopwatch

WHAT TO DO

Dictate a partial or whole scene, where two characters have two different points of view. Don't merely repeat the same actions. Instead, build chronologically, the first half of the scene from one character, the second half from the other, switching POV only once.

As a beginner, you may simply dictate the actions of the scene that drive the plot complication. There will be dialogue.

As an intermediate writer, you should begin pacing the scene with perceptions of the setting shaped by the POV's personality and background.

As an advanced writer, you need to make sure everyone is lying to each other.

Using the timer, cut yourself off at 10 minutes.

PROMPT

The scene began just as...

...Tom returned to the store merely for his forgotten wallet, but Nancy insisted it was for something more.

PRACTICAL EXERCISE #8: 9000 WPH MAYHEM

OBJECTIVE

To stretch the limits of your articulation, as well as your imagination's speed.

YOU'LL NEED

- your dictation setup: *Dragon*, mic, voice recorder, word processor
- stopwatch
- your distraction of choice

WHAT TO DO

Dictate several *narrative* paragraphs in 5 minutes, relating the actions leading up to the event of the prompt—while trying to maintain a pace of 9000 words per hour.

Think of this as a legitimate scene, including a POV character, his/her objective, an obstacle, and a viable setting that conveys mood. When you read the prompt, mull it over for a minute, imagining as many of those details as you can. You'll be able to think of a lot in a minute.

The only restriction? No inner monologue.

5 minutes of dictation at 9000 WPH churns out 750 words. That's ridiculous. So don't expect fine art. Instead, expect to stretch your dictation skills by getting out of your comfort zone—like a portrait artist expanding her perspective by finger painting.

This practical exercise is a lot like finger painting.

Okay, no. It's *sort of* like finger painting.

This isn't a stream of consciousness exercise. You'll start with an ending point. That's the prompt. It's your job to come up with the events leading up to the prompt. That said, at this pace, you'll occasionally dictate some seriously whacky things that come out of the blue.

Your articulation, breathing, and creative flow state will suffer dramatically, and consequently so will the quality of your dictation. Oh well. Try to think ahead as you dictate. **If you're going to dictate anything meaningful, your imagination must stay one step in front of your tongue.** That's the challenge.

Are you up for it?

Then, start your recorder.

Start the 5-minute timer.

Shoot for 750 words.

Afterwards, transcribe. Log your WPH.

Remember the one rule: no inner monologue.

PROMPT

Show the events just before...

...the exhausted grandmother swipes the money.

PRACTICAL EXERCISE #9: FLASH FICTION

OBJECTIVE

To improvise short fiction that includes a beginning, middle, and end.

YOU'LL NEED

- your dictation setup: *Dragon*, mic, voice recorder, word processor
- stopwatch

WHAT TO DO

Dictate a short story containing less than 500 words within 5 minutes. Dictate the same one twice for a total of 10 minutes. The story must have some version of:

1. a set-up, revealing the background & status quo

2. a catalyst, causing the protagonist to do something beyond the status quo
3. an obstacle, challenge, or threat
4. an action by the protagonist that changes everything
5. a wrap-up, revealing the new status quo

Flash fiction can be great because there are no rules. Then again, flash fiction can be awful for the same reason. Therefore, you have the above guidelines to keep you on track. Use them for this exercise.

As usual, the result you're working toward isn't a story to share. It's the skills you develop while doing it over and over. Paint the fence, Daniel-san. Here, your dictating brain will begin aligning with the part of your brain that knows story composition. In a short format, you'll dictate the rhythms of story. The beginning, middle, and end. The opening, the development, and the conclusion.

If you want to stretch your abilities *after you're comfortable with the basics*, then try composing your short story in a non-linear fashion.

Dictate each story twice, allowing the first attempt to be a brainstorming, exploratory session.

Set the timer for timer for 5 minutes.

Afterwards, transcribe and log.

Prompts are the sensational titles of your story. Give yourself a minute or two with each title before you begin recording. Run down the components numbered above.

PROMPT

- He Was A Teenaged Robot

PRACTICAL EXERCISE #10:
INCREMENTAL SCENES

OBJECTIVE

To build scenes layer upon layer, building your confidence to compose scenes with style and rhythm.

YOU'LL NEED

- your dictation setup: *Dragon*, mic, voice recorder, word processor
- stopwatch
- your distraction of choice

WHAT TO DO

Dictate a scene using a simple outline, expanding its details and length in incremental rounds. The first round is 2 minutes. The second is 3 minutes. And the third is 5 minutes.

Here are the steps, the same as those from your Tryout #3.

Step 1. Read the prompt and imagine the scene in your head. Close your eyes and visualize the entire short scene, beginning to end, behind the eyes of the POV character, generating the scene's details. Do this two times.

Step 2. Start the recorder. Set the timer for 2 minutes. Dictate the scene, following the basic outline as best as you can, filling in setting details, character details, and other actions as you go. Stay calm. Speak slowly. But cut yourself off when the timer buzzes, finished or not. Don't transcribe yet. Shake it off.

[*Remember the guidelines for punctuation. Include all punctuation except quotation marks. Say "new line" at the beginning of every paragraph. Skip emphasis fonts, such as italics, underlines, and caps.*]

Step 3. This time, set the timer for 3 minutes. Dictate the scene again. Use those details from step two that you remember. This time, squeeze in a proper ending, more valuable details, more actions that speak to the characters' motivations. Try your best to speak at that slow 5000 WPH pace. At the buzzer, stop and shake it off. Still no transcribing.

Step 4. Set the timer for 5 minutes. Do it again. But this time, try to have fun. Breathe. Enlarge one scene beat. Shrink another. Feel it out. Use details you remember from the other two steps. Don't worry if you can't recall them all. That's one of the reasons you're recording. Create more details and more actions to fill in the time. Don't go past the buzzer.

Step 5. Transcribe all three attempts. Log word counts.

Step 6. Edit all three attempts into a single version of the scene.

Limiting yourself to 2 scenes per session. Aim for quality instead of quantity.

For fiction writers, every scene must be worth the reader's time, always pushing forward the plot, always developing the emotional progression of the characters, always bonding those characters to the reader. Fiction writers must master their scene writing process.

Be in charge of your scenes. Own them. Feed them. Dominate them with deliberate writing. If you're unsure whether your scenes are good, you need to find a method that puts you in control.

This one practical exercise will, with time and repetition, make you the writing, dictating boss of your scenes. And those scenes will work well for you.

Below is your first prompt. Invent as much backstory as you need, and you will have lots of wiggle room, but remember this is a short scene. **Merely connect the dots of the opening, peak emotional moment, and the ending.** If you get lost during your dictation, move to the next part of the outline. A little jump in time sometimes adds relief to an otherwise linear scene.

Good luck.

Prompt

- **Scene Summary:** Alex went to the old warehouse, looking for his client's satchel, but Sophia arrived, claiming to be the villain's sister.
- **Where:** creepy industrial district, rain
- **Opening:** Alex tried seeing through his fogged windshield if the area was safe.
- **Peak Emotional Moment:** Sophia pulled away from Alex's arms, shouting through the rain that she can't go on: she's the villain's sister!
- **Ending:** Alex threw the satchel in his car, not even caring anymore what was inside.

PART 4

FINAL NOTES

YOUR OWN CONSISTENT PRACTICE

This is where I avoid meddling too much into your life. You know what you want to accomplish. You know your specific time constraints. And you know how disciplined you really are.

However, let's review what will work for you if applied to your own writing career. Primarily, the Fool Proof Dictation system is built around a consistent practice. It includes:

1. reading aloud in a consistent voice that reinforces slow and articulate dictation,
2. solidifying your goals,
3. completing 2 practical exercises per session, 2-3 prompts each,
4. non-disruptive breaks,
5. dictating a complete scene of your WIP, from an outline, in incremental rounds,
6. transcribing those WIP rounds, quickly editing them into a single 1st Draft version,
7. tracking your performance,

8. briefly reflecting on the session, and getting excited about the next one.

If you're only allowed 15 minutes here, 15 minutes there, then work the above elements into your day the best you can. It's doable. But it's harder, for sure. In such cases, your WIP will suffer because it's difficult to get into and stay within the creative flow state. But keep at the practical exercises until you can find a way to gain larger chunks of time.

If you're between projects, continue conducting sessions, albeit shorter ones. A musician doesn't quit playing and practicing just because a performance isn't coming up soon. Keep working the exercises a few times a week. Read aloud when you have spare moments, practicing your target pace.

Professionally, I suggest that you're never between projects. You're a writer. Even if you're a complete novice, you should always be working on something. Even if you're in the outlining stage of your tenth novel, you should be sharpening your dictation skills. Or you should be dabbling in short stories. With the higher words per hour of dictation, you could assemble a collection short stories quickly, even if it's under a pen name in a genre you don't want your regular followers knowing about.

Continually writing viable works of fiction, short stories or novels, keeps the practical exercises in this book from growing tiresome, keeps you stretching for specific goals, keeps you improving for a reason.

This book doesn't discuss dictation accuracy much. Truth is, your accuracy will peak when you develop a calm, consistent pace. This includes thoughtful articulation, deliberate breathing, and regular review of your transcriptions. **In other words, stay calm. Following the Fool Proof Dictation system is about that, helping you stay calm, so all the right parts of your**

brain can do their job. Yes, you'll need to input irregular names and genre specific words into *Dragon*'s vocabulary files. But that's it. Accuracy will come with practice. Fool Proof Dictation keeps you moving forward for that to happen.

Do you have a feeling now that more productive dictation is within your grasp? It is. I look forward to hearing how this adventure goes for you.

If you have any questions or feedback, email me at csdowning@mad-devilmedia.net. I'll be available to help.

Good luck on your dictation journey. I hope new doors of creativity and productivity await now that you have the tools to open them. Stay at it.

When you've experienced a few successful sessions, **share you experience as an Amazon review**. Other writers will want to know if Fool Proof Dictation really helps or not, and they'd want to hear your opinion to make an informed purchase!

And happy dictating!

250 PROMPTS!

DON'T FORGET TO REVISIT THE INSTRUCTIONS FOR EACH PRACTICAL EXERCISE OFTEN!

SIMPLE SENTENCES & SIMPLE EDITS

FOR PRACTICAL EXERCISE #1

Modify the words to stay within your genre. And challenge yourself to work around the obvious.

25 PROMPTS

- ecstatic soldier
- train car
- dawn
- locket

- vigilant heiress
- countryside
- thunder
- rope
- bravery

- raging pastor
- small town
- fog
- sacrifice

- hateful merchant
- evil
- cave
- insect

- grieving miner
- hat
- comfort
- baby crib

- amazed government clerk
- beacon
- ship
- flowers

- horrified acrobat
- film set
- snow
- ego

- wind

- social worker in awe
- rough part of town
- heatwave
- justice
- river

- joyful doctor
- forest
- hazy
- coffee
- explosion
- heaven

- eager traitor
- desert island
- thunderstorm
- boat
- defeat

- angry client
- necklace
- attic
- hope

- disgusted cop
- isolation
- gusty
- doll
- burial

- sad veterinarian
- tiger
- compassion
- village

- surprised speech writer
- sunset
- wealthy estate
- cake

- fearful daughter
- snowed-in
- vase
- music player
- thermometer

- trusting lawyer
- ancient

- gravel
- shadow

- disapproving brother
- tavern
- mud
- musk

- cowardly postal carrier
- feral
- raccoon
- geese
- treehouse

- optimistic politician
- rain
- expectations
- saggy
- alone

- aggressive salesman
- talking rabbit
- tornado
- siren
- tea time

- bored psychic
- downtown
- midnight
- voicemail
- 911

- remorseful father
- beach
- dusk
- flower bunch
- wallet

- distracted driver
- text
- raindrops
- pothole
- clown

- apprehensive comic
- whiskey
- spotlight
- empty
- last call

- swooning sports fan
- reclusive sports star
- life raft

To create your own prompts, explore **random item generators** online. Even if they come up with silly combinations, it's better than getting hung up while trying to think of what to dictate about.

When you get to the bottom of the list, feel free to start again, only this time in that genre you've been secretly thinking about.

SENTENCE VARIATIONS V.1

FOR PRACTICAL EXERCISE #2

Remember, first spend 30 seconds thinking of a little story behind each image. Regularly alternate between simple sentences first and compound sentences first.

25 PROMPTS

[Images via Pixabay, CC0 Public Domain]

STREAM OF CONSCIOUSNESS

FOR PRACTICAL EXERCISE #3

You don't need to stay on topic, especially if you can't think of anything to dictate before the 10 minutes are up. If all else fails, talk about the weather. The goal is to let your mind wander while you dictate articulately.

25 PROMPTS

- How's technology more trouble than it's worth?
- Describe an experience that left you disillusioned. Go from there.
- Relate a frightening or dangerous experience.
- What makes a memorable journey?
- Invent an encounter with someone you are either in awe of or afraid of.
- What does rejection feel like? Why?
- Why do people live in big cities?
- Describe watching a friend or relative going through a breakup.

- What if you got everything you wished for?
- Who misunderstands you? Why?
- How do you feel about lying?
- Defend a difficult decision you had to make.
- Describe a turning point in your life. What if it didn't happen?
- Who's an influence on you?
- Do police make you feel safe or nervous?
- What do real life heroes have in common?
- Imagine an encounter with a fictitious person.
- When is rebellion justified?
- Describe the events leading up to a brush with death. If that's never happened, imagine it.
- What's it feel like to take a stand on an important issue? How do you know?
- What things are deal breakers for your friendships?
- Here's a million dollars. What are going to do with it?
- What's your favorite book or movie from childhood? What's changed?
- How does one overcome fear? Any examples from your own life?
- So, how's dictation going for you?

SENTENCE VARIATIONS V.2

FOR PRACTICAL EXERCISE #4

By the way, these are 25 different Johns and Selenas. Their names are the same for simplicity's sake.

25 PROMPTS

- Selena lost a bet to John.
- Selena and John watched a sad movie. Selena was crying.
- John and Selena showed up at an out-of-control party. John didn't want to be there.
- John was hired to spy on Selena.
- Selena and John were buddy cops.
- Selena and John were part of a team, but their constant bickering caused problems.
- Selena had a hangover, but John felt fine.
- John was the superhero and Selena was the sidekick.
- John got revenge on Selena.
- John and Selena met at a bar. Selena gets too drunk, and John was obligated to take her home.

- Selena was John's bodyguard.
- John helped Selena with chores. She didn't want help but couldn't be honest.
- John and Selena went on a road trip.
- John and Selena pretended *not* to be married for an undercover mission.
- A zombie bit Selena. John had to put her down.
- John got amnesia and forgot everything about Selena.
- Selena and John were the leaders of rival gangs.
- John gave Selena a drunken piggy back ride.
- John revealed a deep, dark, life-long secret to Selena. Selena pretended to care.
- Selena, an agent in body armor, rescued the mistrusting John.
- John and Selena fought over the last piece of cake.
- Fulfilling an ancient prophecy, John was the only mortal able to defeat the evil Selena.
- John saw Selena at a local café every day and fell in love. They never connected.
- Selena struck the finishing blow on John.
- John and Selena were reincarnated lovers, but they weren't compatible this go around.

PERSUASIVE LETTER TO A FRIEND

FOR PRACTICAL EXERCISE #5

No one will call you out if you lie.

25 PROMPTS

At last evening's dinner, your friend insisted the following statement. It's kept you up all night. Do you agree or disagree?

- Grades don't matter!
- Horror movies are good for you!
- Humor makes for better sex!
- The thumb is not a finger!
- Men shouldn't wear skinny jeans!
- My boss should work for me!
- Nice people do not make the world go around!
- Facebook made her smarter!
- Dry cookies/biscuits are barely food!
- Gossip is good for the workplace!
- Free Will is, like, the worst thing ever!
- I need my coffee!

- Clothes do make the man!
- Dogs are better!
- Grass is greener on the other side!
- People should eat more apple pie!
- Teenagers deserve a chance!
- Tanning says a lot about a person!
- Advertising works!
- Global warming makes us a stronger species in the long run!
- Homelessness gets a bad rap!
- Chewing gum is the bane of civilized society!
- There's a correct way to make pancakes!
- Zippers cause laziness!
- Freedom of speech does have one regrettable downfall!

When you run out of prompts, search for news. It's not hard finding screwball people making screwball assertions. Or test your creative irony by creating your own.

SENTENCE VARIATIONS V.3

FOR PRACTICAL EXERCISE #6

Try to make it interesting. Highlight mundane details that reveal significant details about you.

25 Prompts

How do you...

1. ...pour a glass of juice?
2. ...put on your shoes?
3. ...drive to the store?
4. ...feed a pet?
5. ...enter your workplace?
6. ...contact a friend?
7. ...butter a muffin?
8. ...select an outfit?
9. ...call for the waiter?
10. ...water the plants?
11. ...convince someone to watch your movie pick?
12. ...pay the bills?
13. ...read a book?

14. ...choose a sandwich from the menu?
15. ...cross a busy street?
16. ...get focused to write?
17. ...boil water?
18. ...stay in touch with family?
19. ...pretend you like someone's quiche?
20. ...get ready for bed?
21. ...exercise?
22. ...prepare for the zombie apocalypse?
23. ...enjoy a sunset?
24. ...shop for jeans?
25. ...show love?

ALTERNATING POVS

FOR PRACTICAL EXERCISE #7

The many alternate universes of Tom and Nancy.

25 PROMPTS

The scene begins just as...

...Tom admitted he was a different species of alien than Nancy had thought all along.

...Tom blackmailed Nancy over those indecent photos from the company party.

...Nancy realized everything was a hallucination, while Tom sat at her bedside in the hospital.

...Tom discovered everyone else was actually plotting against Nancy, and she wouldn't believe him.

...Nancy and Tom discovered the world was dependent on magic—and Nancy had it!

...Nancy turned out to be Tom's aunt.

...Nancy admitted she needed the drug or she'd die. Tom pretended he didn't have money to get it.

...Nancy and Tom discovered humans were secretly infested with nanotechnology. Nancy was disgusted. Tom thought it was awesome.

...Tom, who didn't want to be a psychic, proved to Nancy that he was. Nancy, who did want to be a psychic, didn't believe him, proving that she, in fact, wasn't.

...Nancy learned Tom swindled candy from the neighbor kids. Regularly.

...Tom and Nancy figured out that the clothes they sold from their shop was, despite their marketing campaign, made in squalid sweatshops.

...Tom turned out to be Nancy's uncle. Which meant their wedding was definitely off.

...Nancy admitted how much she hated Tom's sister.

...Nancy and Tom learned that all their memories together were implanted.

...The mysterious briefcase was discovered. Tom wanted to take it to the cops. Nancy wanted to open it.

...Tom realized halfway through his marriage proposal that Nancy was totally stoned.

...Nancy went in for the cuddle, but Tom went for chips.

...Nancy began telling Tom that his father was to blame for the fire. Tom wanted to believe her.

...The alien invasion totally ruined Tom and Nancy's cruise.

...Nancy accidentally kissed Tom. It was meant for his brother.

...Tom said, "If you want the ring so damn bad, put your hand in the garbage disposal. See what happens." Nancy did.

...Nancy and Tom realized the plane is going down. The pilot and the chute were gone.

...Tom discovered, despite all the evidence, that Nancy was innocent. Nancy wasn't nice about it.

...Nancy and Tom discussed how much her cat's surgery would cost.

...Tom finally showed Nancy his powers as the grand sorcerer of ancient Agrabath. Nancy just wanted to get the groceries put away before the ice cream melted.

9000 WPH MAYHEM

FOR PRACTICAL EXERCISE #8

Remember, the prompt is the ending point of your narrative. Stay away from inner monologue.

25 PROMPTS

Show the events just before...

1. ...the priest stops the wedding.
2. ...the burnt-out actor boards the train.
3. ...the astrophysicist pushes the red button.
4. ...the rookie cop pulls the trigger.
5. ...the artistic mobster orders the hit.
6. ...the self-conscious world-champ call the speech therapist.
7. ...the hunter knocks on the cabin door.
8. ...the gambler calls her husband.
9. ...the rootin' tootin' bandit dies in the dirt.
10. ...the woman takes a drink after three years.
11. ...the murderer confesses to a random child.
12. ...the soldier almost gets hit.

13. ...mean-spirited teacher helps the student.
14. ...the IT technician hands over the flash drive for cash.
15. ...the freshman asks out the senior.
16. ...the homeless architect nabs the job.
17. ...the fighter pilot turns in his wings.
18. ...the self-righteous popstar loses a fist-fight.
19. ...the fire-fighter makes the leap.
20. ...the lawyer falls asleep in his car.
21. ...the cat reveals the imposter.
22. ...the male CEO fires his male assistant.
23. ...the female CEO fires her female assistant.
24. ...the elderly professor walks out on the class.
25. ...the tireless writer gets the big contract.

FLASH FICTION

FOR PRACTICAL EXERCISE #9

Flash fiction meets 1950's pulp fiction. Have fun!

25 PROMPTS

1. Bettie the Lizard Master Rides Again
2. Tears of the Executioner
3. Ken Doll Unbound
4. Mission Delta
5. My Dad Married Medusa
6. The Wizard's Choice
7. The Bone Healers
8. The Dinosaur Zombie Attacks
9. The Mad Professor from Beyond
10. The Terrible Legend of the Steve
11. Tornado 2017
12. Voyage Beyond Pluto
13. The Gladiator's Wife
14. Breed Hunters

15. Disease of the Innocents
16. Insanity Office
17. My Mom Married Your Mom
18. Odyssey to Mars
19. Trials of The Elephant-Women
20. The Bloody Paul Roberts
21. The Body Trappers
22. The Cannibal in the KGB
23. The Unbelievable Case of Robert Jones
24. The Cyborgs from Beyond
25. Scorpion-Women from The Future

INCREMENTAL SCENES

FOR PRACTICAL EXERCISE #10

None of these scenes are related. Sure would be an interesting novel if they were!

Remember, these are short scenes. Don't get lost in your head. Just follow the outline. Connect the dots.

25 Prompts

- **Scene Summary**: Sophia wanted to reach Alex before the bomb went off, but the crowd was too dense, and she was too late.
- **Where**: the music festival, high noon
- **Opening:** Sophia took her first bite of a hotdog at the concession stand, noticing something amiss.
- **Peak Emotional Moment**: Sophia watched helplessly as flames and smoke burst at the side of the stage.
- **Ending**: Sophia got trampled as the crowd panicked.

- **Scene Summary:** Alex wanted to make the meeting on time, but his legs couldn't go any further.
- **Where:** City sidewalk, daytime
- **Opening:** Alex hung up the phone with his boss, who was waiting for him.
- **Peak Emotional Moment:** After running for ten minutes, Alex realized he wouldn't make it.
- **Ending:** Alex, missing a shoe, sweaty, and furious, fought back the tears.

- **Scene Summary:** Sophia wanted to help at Alex's mobile soup kitchen, but he turned her away because of her age.
- **Where:** crowded inner city park, fading light, cold
- **Opening:** Through the chain fence, Sophia nervously watched the long line at the food truck.
- **Peak Emotional Moment:** Alex barked at her to get away from the crowds, to get where it's safe.
- **Ending:** Sophia sat in the driver's seat, waiting for Alex to finish, realizing how naive she was.

- **Scene Summary:** Sophia wanted to rappel into the cave, but Alex kept insisting the rope wouldn't hold.
- **Where:** Tropical forest, isolated, drizzly
- **Opening:** Sophia walked up on Alex, who was fussing over the rope and the knot.
- **Peak Emotional Moment:** Sophia told Alex not to come, to stay away from the damn rope, to go back home without the treasure if that's what he wanted.

- **Ending:** Sophia watched Alex's silhouette shrink at the rim as she descended, watched him pull out a knife, watched him turn and walk out of view.

- **Scene Summary:** Alex wanted to pout in his room, but he found a tiny alien flying saucer on his windowsill instead.
- **Where:** Alex's room, posters and toys, dinnertime
- **Opening:** Alex slammed his door and sat at his desk, grumbling.
- **Peak Emotional Moment:** The little alien said he was looking for a super hero, and Alex lied, saying it was him.
- **Ending:** The little alien said he'd be back in three days to take him to the alien's home world.

- **Scene Summary:** Alex wanted to enjoy the beach, but Sophia showed up, getting pushy.
- **Where:** Sandy beach, beautiful day
- **Opening:** Alex kicked off his dress shoes, unbuttoned his shirt, and sat in the sand.
- **Peak Emotional Moment:** Sophia yelled, "Is this what I pay you for?" and Alex stood up to her, shouted her down, told her "What I do on my time is my own business!"
- **Ending:** Sophia plopped on the sand and burst into tears, playing the damsel in distress card, while Alex watched the sailboats in the distance.

- **Scene Summary:** Alex wanted to apologize to Sophia for snubbing her boss at the party, but she wouldn't stop shopping.
- **Where:** Macy's, five minutes before closing
- **Opening:** Alex finally broke the ice through the door of the changing room, bringing up last night.
- **Peak Emotional Moment:** Alex grabs Sophia's wrist as she reaches for a blouse on the rack, barking, "Hey, I'm trying to say sorry!"
- **Ending:** Alex tries to stare down the security guard but can't, glancing at Sophia as she walks away.

- **Scene Summary:** Alex waited for his brother to show up, but the hitman pulled up instead.
- **Where:** Outside the crowded nightclub, midnight
- **Opening:** Alex felt the awkward weight of the pistol in his jacket pocket.
- **Peak Emotional Moment:** The car that was supposed to bring his brother was exited by the Croatian with the shotgun.
- **Ending:** Alex tossed the pistol in a dumpster a block away, frightened for his brother's life.

- **Scene Summary:** Sophia wanted to make Alex tell her the location of the secret base.
- **Where:** The abandoned mansion in the country, daytime, thunderclouds
- **Opening:** Sophia slowly descended the stairs for dramatic effect.

- **Peak Emotional Moment:** Alex spat the kerosene back in Sophia's face, insisting his ignorance.
- **Ending:** Sophia's husband knocked the lighter from her hand, told her she's gone to far.

- **Scene Summary:** Alex wanted to tell his sister that the villain was their long lost brother.
- **Where:** Sidewalk cafe, overcast, lunch
- **Opening:** Alex fidgeted with small talk at the table, while Sophia got annoyed.
- **Peak Emotional Moment:** Alex finally blurted, "That crime boss is our brother!" to which Sophia mumbled, "I know, you idiot."
- **Ending:** Alex, distrusting everyone now, crawled out the cafe's bathroom window.

- **Scene Summary:** Alex stepped in to protect the attendant, but Sophia turned on him.
- **Where:** The psychiatric ward, 3 AM
- **Opening:** Dr. Alex heard a scuffle down the hall.
- **Peak Emotional Moment:** As Dr. Alex tried to pull Sophia off the nurse, Sophia turned her wrath on him, punching and kicking.
- **Ending:** Dr. Alex sat on the floor, wiping the blood from his nose and lip, watching the crowd of burly nurses administer the sedative.

- **Scene Summary:** Sophia wanted to make a birthday cake for Alex, but she'd never baked before.
- **Where:** Alex's kitchen, during the day
- **Opening:** Sophia told Alex to have a great day at work, closing the front door.
- **Peak Emotional Moment:** Covered in flour and tears, Sophia broke down, realizing she didn't know what she was doing, in the kitchen and in the relationship.
- **Ending:** Sophia admitted defeat, slowly wiping up the mess.

- **Scene Summary:** During his second date with Sophia, Alex wanted the neighbors to turn the music down, but he was too timid.
- **Where:** Alex's little apartment, warm evening
- **Opening:** Alex and Sophia just finished a nice dinner, and Alex put on *Annie Hall*.
- **Peak Emotional Moment:** Sophia finally took charge, knocked on the neighbors' door, and effectively got the music dropped—without any major conflict.
- **Ending:** Alex began drinking too much wine, and Sophia declared she never liked *Annie Hall*.

- **Scene Summary:** Alex wanted to go to corner store for a six-pack, but robbers messed up his plan.
- **Where:** City sidewalk, late at night, chilly wind
- **Opening:** Alex stepped from the doorway of his building, tightening against the cold.
- **Peak Emotional Moment:** Without a second thought,

Alex snatched the gun from the boy's hand and bent him over the counter. Then, his heart rate jumped.

- **Ending:** The pleas of gratitudes from the clerk fading behind him in the wind, Alex tucked the gun under his arm, not knowing why he'd keep it. But he did.

- **Scene Summary:** Sophia wanted to buy the popcorn, but Alex kept insisting he buy everything.
- **Where:** The mall movie theater, after school
- **Opening:** Alex and Sophia at the movies "as friends," and Alex just bought the tickets.
- **Peak Emotional Moment:** At the candy counter, Sophia whispers too quietly for Alex to understand, "You're going to ruin this, aren't you?"
- **Ending:** Sophia pretended to receive a text from home, leaving dumbfounded Alex with the ticket puncher at the top of the stairs.

- **Scene Summary:** Sophia stole the golden monkey, but Lt. Alex chased her down.
- **Where:** Smithsonian special exhibit gallery
- **Opening:** Sophia lingered in the crowd, made eye contact with the plainclothes cop, but knew she had go through with it because the villain had her brother.
- **Peak Emotional Moment:** Sophia cracked Alex in the head with the statue, knowing she was significantly escalating her crime, the crowd shrieking.
- **Ending:** Alex tackled Sophia, quickly subduing her, then

said, "You're definitely no thief. What the heck are you doing?"

- **Scene Summary:** Sophia thundered down the road toward the postal station, but the wheel of her wagon broke too far away.
- **Where:** The Old American West, light snow
- **Opening:** Sophia cracked the whip over the heads of the horses, the letter tucked in her belt.
- **Peak Emotional Moment:** After being thrown to the cold, hard ground, Sophia rose to stare at the distant town in valley, helpless.
- **Ending:** Sophia clutched the letter in hand, seething with grief and anger...just as Alex rode up on his Morgan.

- **Scene Summary:** Captain Sophia followed the squid-creature's trail into the seedy dive bar, but Alex had already transformed back into a human disguise.
- **Where:** Dark, rough tavern on Space Station Muna-5
- **Opening:** CPT Sophia eyed the slimy tracks that went into the main port of the crowded bar, a dangerous place to go into alone.
- **Peak Emotional Moment:** At the end of the bar, blaster drawn, CPT Sophia confronted the big ruffian in the overcoat, who stared into his drink too long.
- **Ending:** CPT Sophia was held by two thugs as Alex let his tentacles drop out of his coat, telling her she was in big trouble now.

- **Scene Summary:** Alex and Sophia tried the key to the old trunk, but the lock wouldn't open, which is when the little gremlin appeared.
- **Where:** Grandpa's woodshed, dawn, before anyone else was awake
- **Opening:** Alex urged Sophia to hurry across the backyard.
- **Peak Emotional Moment:** The kids finally calmed down when the gremlin called them both by name.
- **Ending:** The gremlin heard a noise, and vanished when the kids looked away. But the key was gone!

- **Scene Summary:** Sophia waited to be questioned at the police station, handcuffed, but when the officers come in, she recognizes one.
- **Where:** Immaculate interview room, two way mirror and all
- **Opening:** Sophia stared at her hands, cuffed in her lap, and she thought of the killers who would want to frame her, as she was one of the witnesses.
- **Peak Emotional Moment:** Sophia's heart sank when one of those killers walked in, turned out being a cop was his day job.
- **Ending:** She'd not said a single word to their questions, but the cop winked at her, to let know she was doomed.

- **Scene Summary:** Alex tested his powers for the first time, but the reporter spotted him.
- **Where:** Junkyard, heavy rain
- **Opening:** Alex climbed over the fence into the abandoned junkyard, slipping on the wet metal.
- **Peak Emotional Moment:** Alex looked around, took a deep breath, then used his super powers for the first time.
- **Ending:** Just as he was calming down, he noticed movement in his periphery. It was Sophia, that nosey reporter!

- **Scene Summary:** Sophia went to her dad's house to tell him she was going to enter the race, no matter what, but he hated the idea.
- **Where:** Her dad's kitchen, her childhood home, sunny day.
- **Opening:** Sophia pulled off her helmet and looked up the stairs to the front door.
- **Peak Emotional Moment:** Sophia finally just said the words, "Dad, I'm riding in tomorrow's race." Her dad shut her down with "Your mother's dying wish was for me to keep you off the track."
- **Ending:** Sophia put helmet back on, again looking up the stairs to the front door, but her dad was no longer there.

- **Scene Summary:** Alex and Sophia tried to tell her mom that they were in love, but Sophia's mom didn't want to hear it.
- **Where:** Fancy restaurant, crooner at the piano

- **Opening:** Alex and Sophia kept giving each other encouraging looks as the hostess sat them down at the table.
- **Peak Emotional Moment:** Sophia's mother blew up with anxiety, said, "But I never loved your father one bit and that worked out just fine. What's love got to do with it?"
- **Ending:** Alex scooted Sophia out as she yelled, "You ruined everything! Just like this!"

- **Scene Summary:** Alex ran into the farmhouse, looking for the French girl, but the Nazis are closing in.
- **Where:** French countryside, WWII
- **Opening:** Alex watched the last German truck pull away from the edge of the forest.
- **Peak Emotional Moment:** Alex flung open the closet door, revealing a crouched Sophia pointing a pistol right at him.
- **Ending:** Holding hands, they ran back into the forest, toward his hidden jeep.

- **Scene Summary:** Sophia wanted to sell her engagement ring, but Alex refused to buy it.
- **Where:** Pawn shop, 1956
- **Opening:** Sophia watched the people going in and out of the pawn shop, fingering the diamond ring in her hands, contemplating her dreadful newfound poverty.
- **Peak Emotional Moment:** Alex refused to take the ring, giving her 50 dollars instead, along with plenty of discomforting compliments and a promise to see her again.
- **Ending:** The rain began as she walked back to her flat

with the money, regretting everything, wondering what all this was supposed to imply.

- **Scene Summary:** Alex returned to Sophia's apartment to get the last of his stuff, but Sophia wanted a second chance.
- **Where:** Sophia's apartment, after work
- **Opening:** Alex stared at the door before he knocked, thinking how long he'd been on the other side of it, really wanting to just forget the whole thing.
- **Peak Emotional Moment:** Sophia declared, "But he didn't mean anything to me!"
- **Ending:** Alex was halfway down the elevator when he realized, damn, he forgot his box of stuff after all.

- **Scene Summary:** Alex and Sophia promise to stay friends forever.
- **Where:** Under the bleachers, after the graduation ceremony
- **Opening:** Alex slid down the side of the bleachers, just to visit for the last time the place where he and Sophia had skipped class so many times. She was there.
- **Peak Emotional Moment:** They embrace, without words.
- **Ending:** Sophia's dad called her name, and she darted away.